DAVE MATTHEWS BAND

JUST THE RIFFS

Photography by Danny Clinch

ISBN 1-57560-148-6

Visit our website at www.cherrylane.com

DAVE MATTHEWS BAND

JUST THE RIFFS

INTRODUCTION

From its early days on the Charlottesville, Virginia, club scene to its current arena-headlining tours, the Dave Matthews Band represents a striking pop success story. The band's grass-roots approach has allowed it to parlay its loyal East Coast following from the early '90s into ever-growing successes worldwide, evidenced by sell-out shows around the world, opening slots for the Rolling Stones, album sales consistently in the millions, and numerous Grammy nominations. This is a band that stands out from the horde of would-be alternatives, with the most original sound to emerge in the decade—not surprising, considering the unique and talented mix of jazz-trained and classically-trained musicians that comprise the group. Seldom are such disparate influences (ranging from Cajun to African pop, bluegrass to jazz) synthesized with such artistic flair—the sound is always natural, footloose, and without pretense.

This book features over 45 examples of the band's pan-cultural sound . . . and not only Matthews' guitar parts: Solos and licks from violinist Boyd Tinsley and saxophonist Leroi Moore (many for the first time in a guitar publication) are well represented, as well as guests such as Matthews' long-time guitar companion Tim Reynolds and banjoist extraordinaire Bela Fleck. When you play, study, and absorb these riffs you will experience, firsthand, the genuine passion that is ever-present in the Dave Matthews Band's music.

— **Arthur Rotfeld**

DAVE MATTHEWS BAND
JUST THE RIFFS

CONTENTS

The Best Of What's Around

Words and Music by David J. Matthews

from *Under The Table And Dreaming*

■ Bridge Riff

"The Best Of What's Around" is in A major, but this riff oscillates between a funky, percussive part in A minor and a gentle, care-free part in A major.

`0:39`

What Would You Say

Words and Music by David J. Matthews

Copyright © 1994 Colden Grey, Ltd. (ASCAP)
International Copyright Secured All Rights Reserved

from *Under The Table And Dreaming*

■ Intro Riff

You might find this riff easier to play if you use your thumb to fret the notes that occur on the low E string. In addition to playing each guitar part individually, try both combined in a composite part—it's possible and not too difficult!

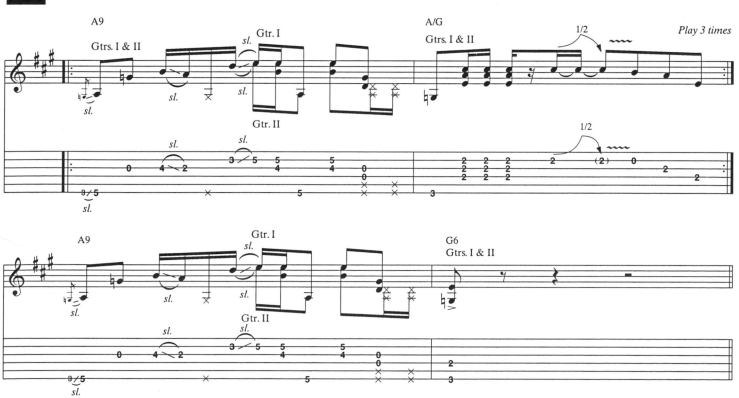

■ Break Riff

Notice the effective and subtle oblique motion between the A7sus4 and the A7—both outer voices remain on pitch, while the higher, inside voice D moves down to C♯. The remainder of the riff is Funk Guitar 101: chock full of sliding 9th chords, octave licks, and single-note fills.

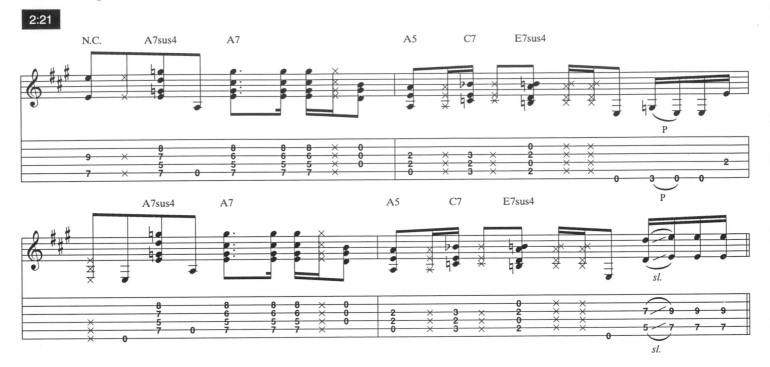

Satellite

Words and Music by David J. Matthews

from *Under The Table And Dreaming*

■ Intro Riff

This riff is mainly comprised of 5ths played on adjacent strings, and as such it makes a good stretching exercise. You'll need to keep your left-hand thumb centered on the back of the neck (just like your guitar teacher told you) to play this figure comfortably. Notice that the grouping of the eighth notes is in a 3+2+2+2+3 pattern.

■ Chorus Riff

The textures of these two guitars contrast each other greatly—one with whimsical trebly fingerpicking, and the other, a low, rhythmically decisive part. There is careful voice leading in both guitar parts: notes that are common to successive chords tend to be held, while those notes that change tend to move to notes that are nearby.

Rhyme & Reason

Words and Music by David J. Matthews

from *Under The Table And Dreaming*

■ Intro Riff

This riff shares the same aesthetic as the Intro Riff from "Satellite," but here the eighth notes are grouped in a 3+3+2 pattern, and 4ths and 6ths are the prominent intervals.

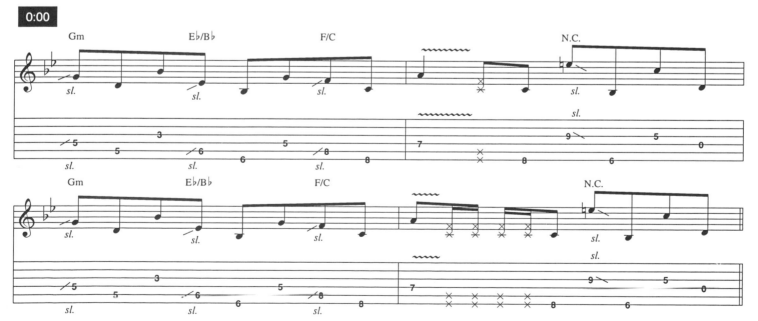

Typical Situation

Words and Music by David J. Matthews

from *Under The Table And Dreaming*

■ Intro/Verse Riff

A two-note ostinato (G and B) is played over changing bass notes in this meditative riff. The G and B sound as the 3rd and 5th of an Em chord when played over the E bass note, but function as the 5th and 7th of a Cmaj7 chord when played over the C bass note.

■ Chorus Riff

The more active rhythms in the guitar and the faster *harmonic rhythm* (the rate at which chords change) contribute to the brighter mood that occurs here.

Ants Marching

Words and Music by David J. Matthews

from *Under The Table And Dreaming*

◼ Intro Riff #1

The first of several Boyd-Tinsley violin riffs arranged for guitar in this book. For many, this riff is to the Dave Matthews Band what the "Satisfaction" riff is to the Rolling Stones.

`0:00`

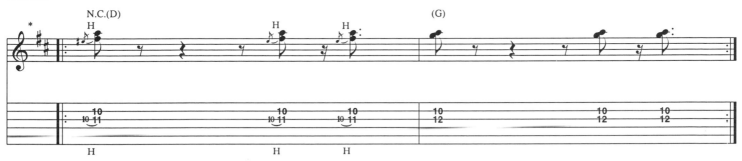

*Violin arr. for gtr.

◼ Intro Riff #2

This is the guitar accompaniment played under Intro Riff #1. Here, Matthews establishes a firm idea in bar 1, then modifies it—only as much is needed—to match the G major harmony in bar 2. Stefan Lessard's bass line lands on the root in the first part of each bar, but then goes on to match Matthew's single-note part.

`0:11`

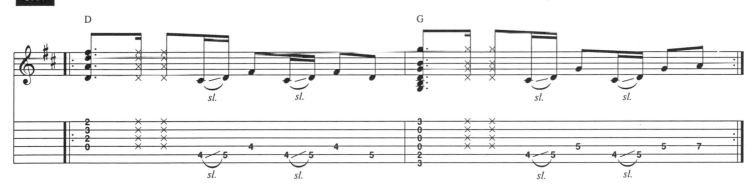

◼ "Take These Chances" Riff

After all the downbeat emphasis of the previous riffs, it's refreshing to hear this (literally) upbeat riff, with most chord changes falling on the "ands" of beats. The underlined characters designate these chord attacks: 1 & 2 & 3 & 4 & | 1 & 2 & 3 & 4 & |.

`1:36`

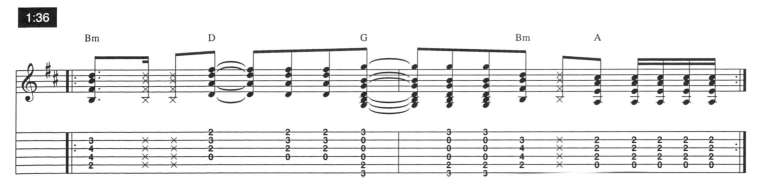

9

"Ants Marching" (Cont.)

◼ Ascending Lick

This violin lick, comprised entirely of stepwise motion, emphasizes important notes on the strong beats: The root (G) and 3rd (B) of the G major chord are attacked on beats 1 and 3 in the second bar, and the root (D) of the D chord is attacked at the downbeat of the third bar.

* Violin arr. for gtr.

◼ Yahoo! . . . The Violin Solo

This great violin break is a fine example of down-home, bluegrass fiddle playing. An integral part of this style is the use of open strings; the violin is tuned in 5ths (G D A E), and Tinsley makes good use of the open D and A. The guitar arrangement here requires that you tune your high E down to D (it will match the pitch of the B string, 3rd fret). Most of this solo lies well on the guitar with this tuning; the hardest part is in the 3rd bar—the best fingering here is to play the first three beats in 7th position and then move to 5th position for the final beat. This means that you'll fret the 6th-fret F♮ with your 2nd finger (use your 1st finger for support!) and fret the 7th-fret A with your 3rd finger.

*Violin arr for gtr.
**Tune high E down to D.

Jimi Thing

Words and Music by David J. Matthews

from *Under The Table And Dreaming*

◼ Intro Riff

This two-guitar riff simultaneously conjures up images of Hendrix in its chord voicings and the Grateful Dead in its rhythmic feel and groove.

0:00

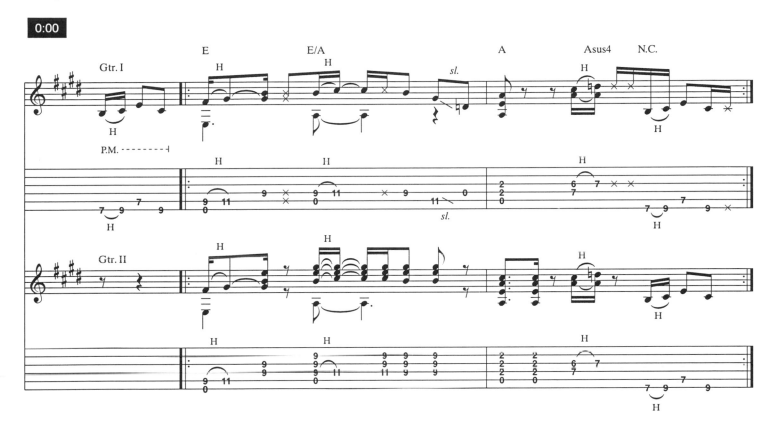

◼ Violin Solo

In contrast to the boot-scooting "Ants Marching" solo, this rocker is even played with distortion! Though this gut-busting extravaganza has all the vigor of a high-energy rock guitar solo, complete with imitation bends (Tinsley uses drawn-out slides to approximate this guitar technique), it is still violinistic, as proved by the use of open strings and marcato bowings (see the beginning of bar 4).

3:19

*Violin arr. for gtr.

11

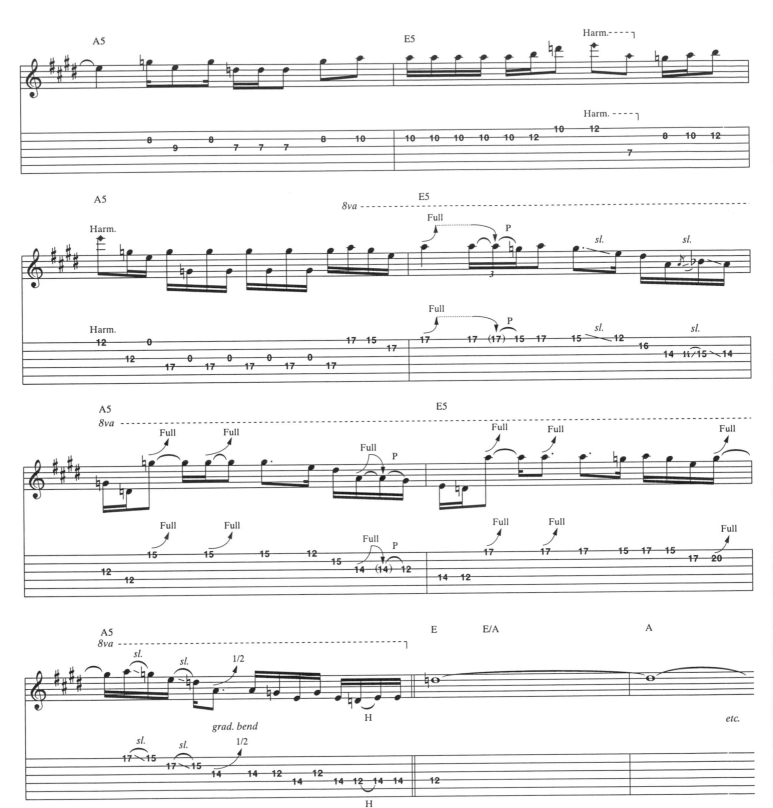

34

Music by David J. Matthews, Leroi Moore,
Carter Beauford and Haines Fullerton

from *from Under The Table And Dreaming*

■ Intro Riff

Not since Andy Summers has a guitarist gotten so much out of the stacked-5ths voicing (A E B, for example). Matthews gives it his own twist by using it in syncopated, compound-meter grooves like this one in ⅝, in contrast to Summer's poppy, simple meter feels in ¼.

0:00

So Much To Say

Words and Music by David J. Matthews, Boyd Tinsley and Peter Griesar

from *Crash*

■ Verse Riff

This riff get its bluesy sound from the C♯ (on the "and" of beat 2 in bars 1, 3, and 4) in what is otherwise an A minor riff and progression.

0:13

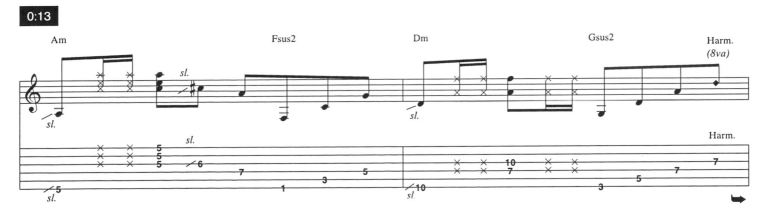

13

"So Much To Say" (Cont.)

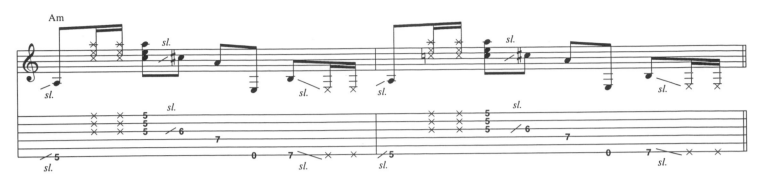

■ Sax Riff

Leroi Moore plays this riff on baritone sax. The highly syncopated, primarily staccato character of Moore's part is 180 degrees from Matthew's lyrical and downbeat-oriented vocal melody.

1:53

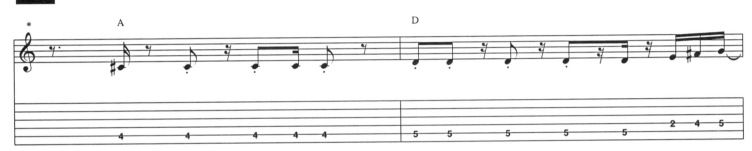

* Sax. arr. for gtr.

Two Step

Words and Music by David J. Matthews

from *Crash*

■ Intro Lick

This simple, elegant melody is comprised of nothing more than a stepwise D minor line played first over an A pedal (in bar 1), and then over a G pedal (in bar 3).

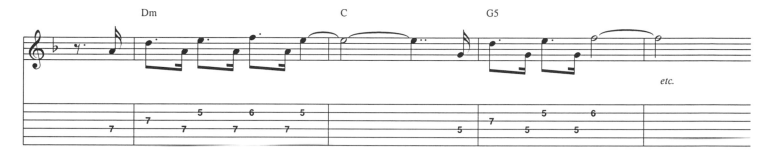

■ Counterpoint Riff

The upstemmed line here is a high, pizzicato line played on violin; the downstemmed line is a low figure played on alto sax. Counterpoint results from the rhythmic and melodic independence of each line.

*Violin arr. gtr.   **Sax arr. for gtr. in Drop D tuning (DADGBE)

Crash Into Me

Words and Music by David J. Matthews

Copyright © 1996 Colden Grey, Ltd. (ASCAP)
International Copyright Secured All Rights Reserved

from *Crash*

◼ Main Riff

This lush chordal riff sounds simple to play, but the left-hand fingering poses some challenges. Each chord must ring as long as possible, and changes between chords should be clean and without a break. Try fingering the 4th-fret B with your pinkie—as this note is present throughout, you'll never have to lift off of it. The only strange fingering is the one used for the E5/B. Here, try using the 1st finger for both 2nd-fret notes; this is done by placing your fingertip between the two strings, as if to fret an imaginary string between the A and D strings.

`0:00`

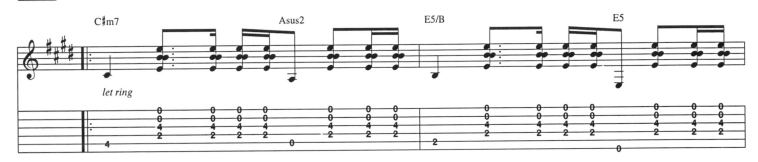

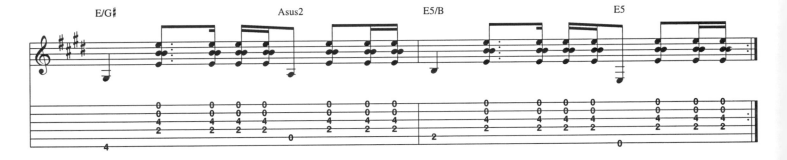

◼ Chorus Riff

This is the airy chorus riff. The quarter note remains constant through these time changes.

 `0:56`

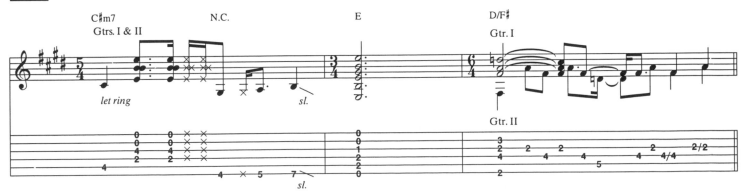

Too Much

Words by David J. Matthews
Music by David J. Matthews, Carter Beauford,
Stefan Lessard, Leroi Moore and Boyd Tinsley

Copyright © 1996 David Matthews, Carter Beauford,
Stefan Lessard, Leroi Moore and Boyd Tinsley (ASCAP)
International Copyright Secured All Rights Reserved

from *Crash*

■ Intro Riff

This intro is in D major, with a surprising B♭ chord at the end (♭Ⅵ in D). The key for the remainder of the song is F♯. The ♭Ⅵ relationship provides a discreet harmonic link between the intro and the body of the song, in that the tonality of the intro, D, is the ♭Ⅵ of F♯!

`0:00`

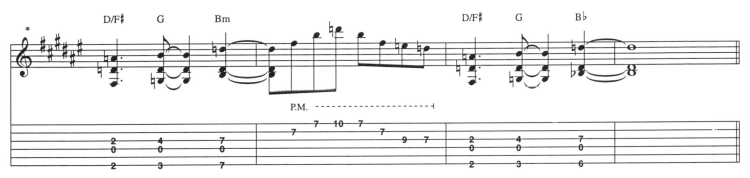

*Two gtrs. arr. for one.

■ Verse Riff

A two-guitar funk dominates the texture here. One guitar plays a gritty, scratch part, while the other plays a somewhat improvisatory, single-note line.

`0:17`

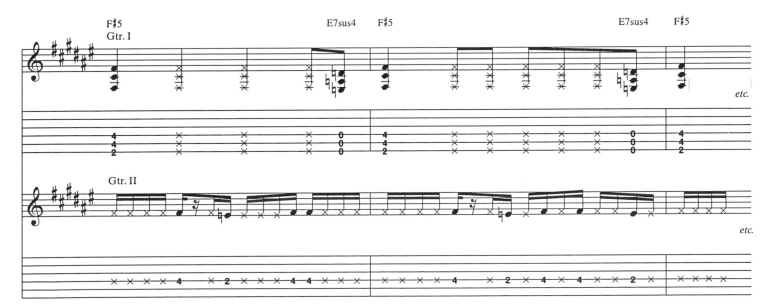

#41

Words by David J. Matthews
Music by David J. Matthews, Carter Beauford,
Stefan Lessard, Leroi Moore and Boyd Tinsley

from *Crash*

■ Intro Riff

This is the basic progression for the intro and verses. You'll note that the lead guitar line (Gtr. I) is expanded and developed throughout. The chords, too, vary from phrase to phrase, but the basic progression, iv–v–i–♭VII, remains intact. Beginning the progression on the iv chord and delaying the i chord until bar 3 creates a more energy-filled progression, one whose harmonic center occurs in the middle of the phrase rather than at the beginning.

■ Verse Riff

This ostinato riff is played on a clean electric. Use a ⊓–∨–∨ picking pattern for the figure on beats 1 and 3.

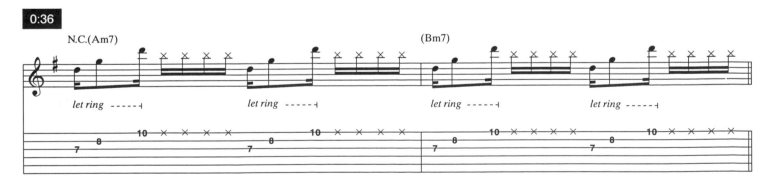

Drive In Drive Out

Words and Music by David J. Matthews

from *Crash*

◼ Intro/Verse Riff

Each bar of this single-note line begins and ends with notes from an A7 chord (A C♯ E G), but the notes in the middle are from a D major chord (D F♯ A).

◼ Chorus Riff

Thickening the texture slightly for the chorus, Matthews plays this octave figure with a tag (bar 4) taken from the Intro/Verse Riff.

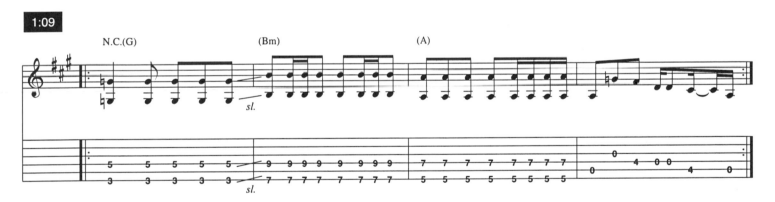

◼ Bridge Riff

This is the basic rhythm guitar part for the bridge, the first three bars of which imply a straight-ahead 3-feel (♩ ♪♪ ♩ in ⅜ = ♩ ♩ ♩ in ¾). Also note the use of a blues-vamp figure in the last two bars.

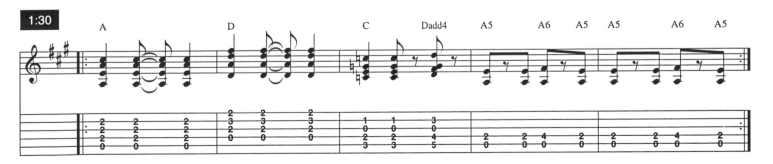

Let You Down

Words by David J. Matthews
Music by David J. Matthews and Stefan Lessard

from *Crash*

■ Main Riff

Here is a prime example of Matthew's trademark lean and widely-spaced voicings. The somewhat nebulous pulse (i.e., where is beat 1?) is achieved by the rhythmic independence of the various instruments combined with the syncopated entrance of each chord in the guitar part.

0:05

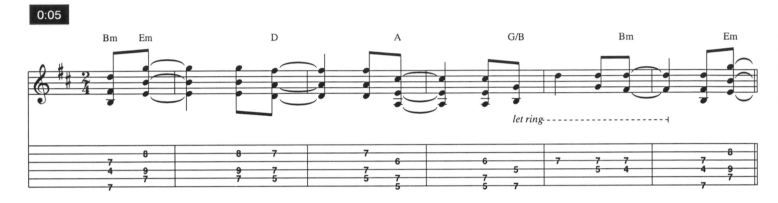

Lie In Our Graves

Words by David Matthews
Music by David Matthews, Carter Beauford,
Stefan Lessard, Leroi Moore and Boyd Tinsley

from *Crash*

■ Intro Riff

This good-time riff includes a smattering of full chords, percussive strokes, single notes, and double-stops. The Bm and Em chords are merely implied, though with the Bm the case is stronger because of the stepwise descent to the B, which falls right on beat 3, and the memory of the D and F♯ from the D chord, which still ring in our mind's ear.

0:00

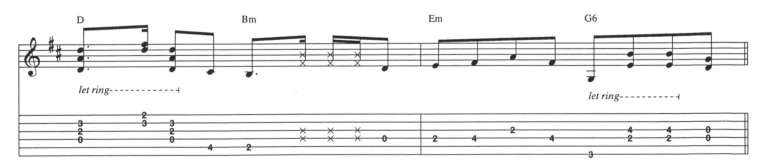

Cry Freedom

Words and Music by David J. Matthews

 Verse Riff

Matthews's simple and elegant playing in this riff shows a true classical sensibility. Note the IV_4^6 chord (a $_4^6$ chord has the 5th in the bass) in bar 2. In classical music, the $_4^6$ chord has three uses: in a cadence (I_4^6–$V7$–I), as a passing chord (I–V_4^6–I^6), or in a pedal section (I–IV_4^6–I). Here, the D/A (IV_4^6) acts as a pedal $_4^6$.

Tripping Billies

Words and Music by David J. Matthews

■ Intro Riff

Even though this intro uses nearly all of the same chords as in "Too Much," it doesn't sound too much like it, thanks to some rhythmic ingenuity.

`0:07`

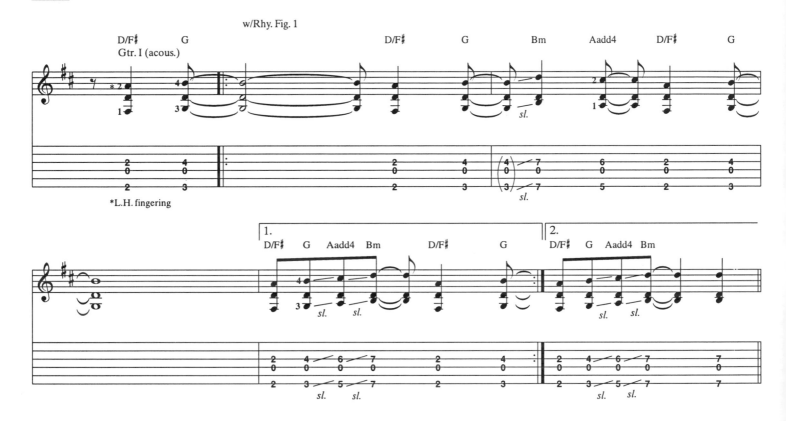

*L.H. fingering

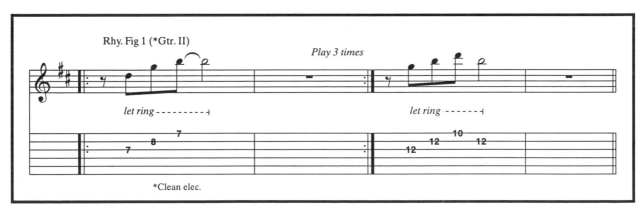

Proudest Monkey

Words by David J. Matthews
Music by David J. Matthews, Carter Beauford,
Stefan Lessard, Leroi Moore and Boyd Tinsley

from *Crash*

■ Guitar Solo

This solo is played on a nylon-string guitar and is comprised of notes from the Ab major scale (Ab Bb C Db Eb F G). As with many major scale–based rock solos, the 7th degree is not often played. In this solo, the 7th (G) is only played once, and even then it's only used as a grace note. A chromatic alteration of the 7th (Gb) is also played as a grace note, in bar 10, for a bluesy effect. Intensity builds throughout the solo via ever-increasing rhythmic activity, but culminates with the double-stops in the final bars.

1:58

*Played behind the beat.

23

"Proudest Monkey" (Cont.)

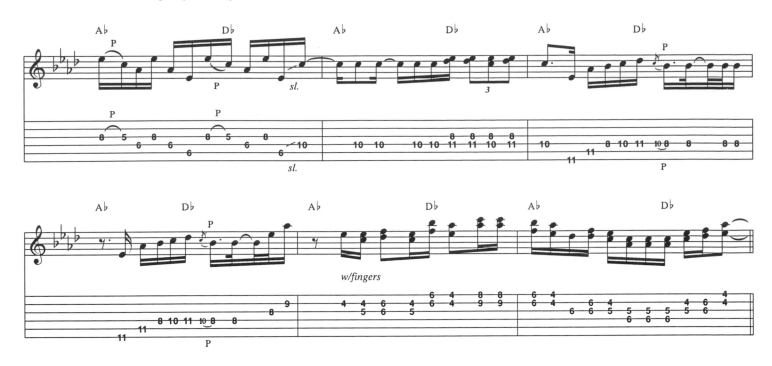

Rapunzel

**Words and Music by David J. Matthews,
Stefan Lessard and Carter Beauford**

from *Before These Crowded Streets*

▓ Intro Riff

This is probably the smoothest funk riff in 5/4 since Led Zeppelin's "The Crunge." Gtr. II is doubled, in spots, by Tinsley's violin.

`0:00`

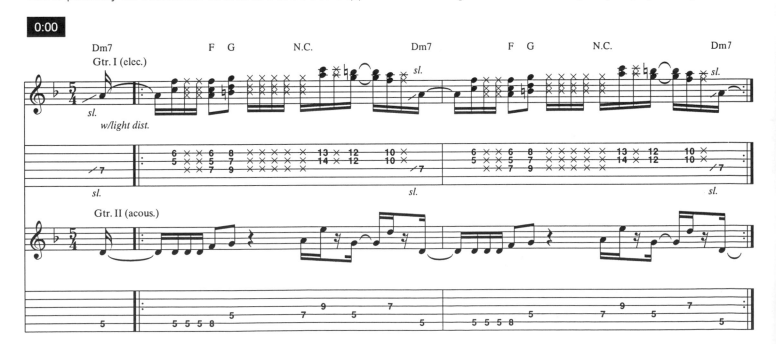

The Last Stop

Words and Music by David J. Matthews and Stefan Lessard

from *Before These Crowded Streets*

▌ Intro Riff

Matthews and Lessard capture a Middle-Eastern vibe here with a Phrygian dominant–based chord progression. F♯ Phrygian dominant (F♯ G A♯ B C♯ D E), the 5th mode of the B harmonic minor scale, is used to generate the harmonies heard here.

`0:00`

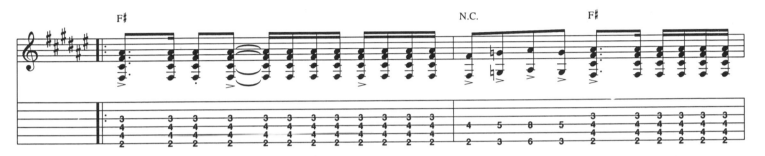

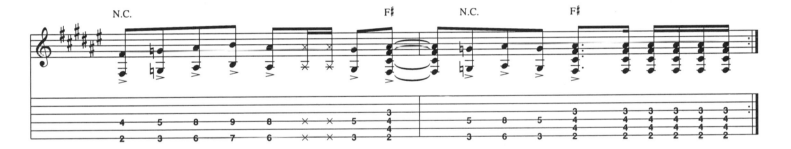

▌ Banjo Rolls

This section, in A major, provides a break from the tension-filled sections that surround it. These arpeggio figures are played by banjoist-extraordinaire Bela Fleck.

`3:09`

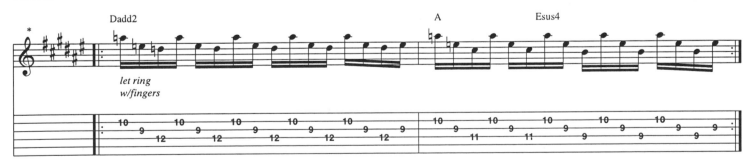

*Banjo arr. for gtr.

Don't Drink The Water

from *Before These Crowded Streets*

◼ Intro Riff

This simple power-chord riff, played in Drop D tuning (D A D G B E), seems to imitate a drum beat: The low D's are bass drum strokes, the accented chords are snare hits, and the sixteenth-note chords are ghost strokes—also played on the snare.

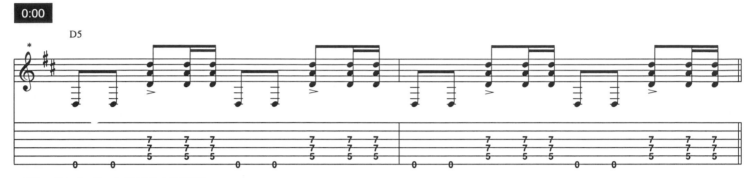

*Drop D tuning (low to high): D A D G B E.

Stay (Wasting Time)

from *Before These Crowded Streets*

◼ Intro Riff

Happy are the two guitars that join together in a bright and jubilant passage such as this one. Take a moment to study the relationship between the two parts, beat by beat—it's not a waste of time.

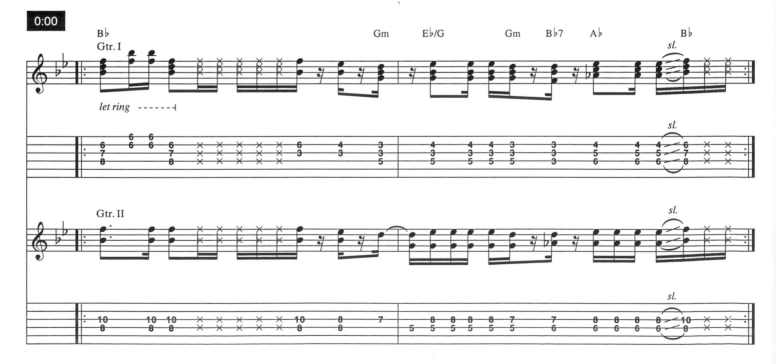

Sax Riff

Leroi Moore lets this soulful figure (bars 1–2) fly and then adds a harmony part (bars 3–4) above it. The notes he uses are from the Bb Mixolydian mode (Bb C Dħ E F G Ab), with an added Db, for good (funky) measure.

*Sax arr. for gtr.

Heavy Guitar Riff

The hard-driving figure is played by two guitars, an octave apart, and bass. If you must choose, play the downstemmed guitar part (Gtr. II), which best represents the thick and forceful nature of the riff.

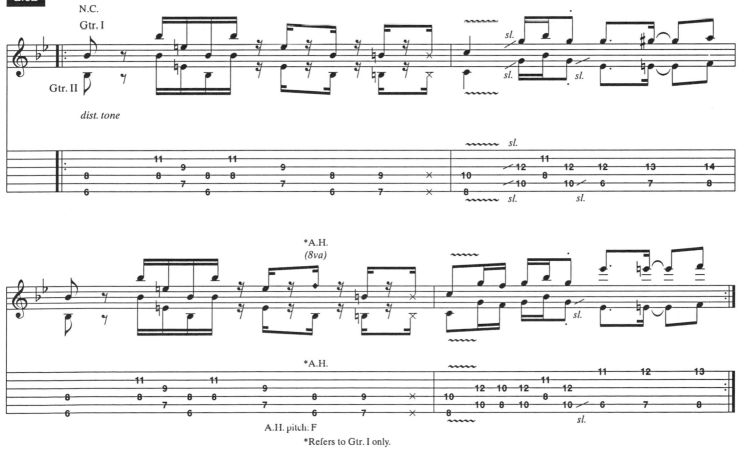

A.H. pitch: F
*Refers to Gtr. I only.

The Stone

Words and Music by David J. Matthews

from *Before These Crowded Streets*

■ Intro Riff

Much like the "Drive In Drive Out" riff, this is an ostinato figure played in § time.

`0:28`

■ Chorus Riff

After all the brooding, D-minor passages, this chorus, in F (the relative major of D minor), is like a breath of fresh air.

`2:36`

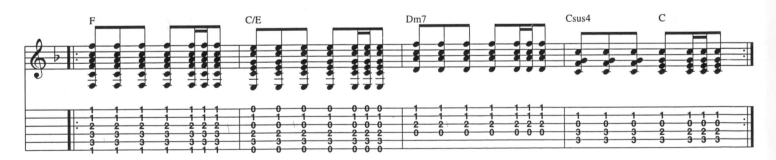

Crush

Words and Music by David J. Matthews

from *Before These Crowded Streets*

Guitar Solo

Tim Reynolds can always be counted on for a well-constructed, organic solo . . . one that flowers naturally from his carefully-sown motivic seeds. Reynolds's tone is strong—slightly overdriven and thick, but not fuzzy or compressed.

"Crush" (Cont.)

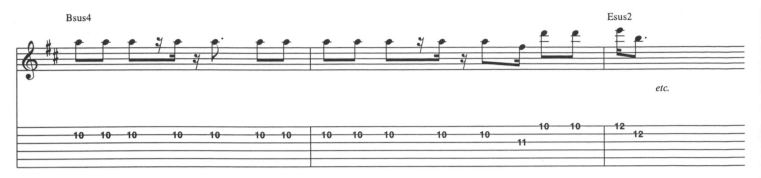

Pig

**Words and Music by David J. Matthews, Stefan Lessard,
Carter Beauford, Leroi Moore and Boyd Tinsley**

*from **Before These Crowded Streets***

■ Interlude Riff

The prevalence of tritones gives this riff a bit of a demonic flair—play it on distorted electric and you might have a Black Sabbath tune!

6:24

Spoon

Words and Music by David J. Matthews

from *Before These Crowded Streets*

Banjo Solo

Throughout this solo, Bela Fleck seems to glide effortlessly through the chord changes, reflecting each harmony in his line. His lick in the final bar is too cool for words.

2:38

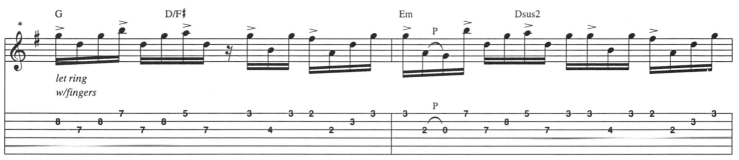

*Banjo arr. for gtr.

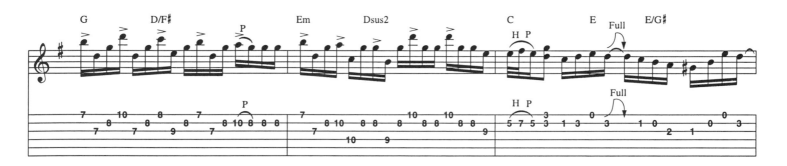

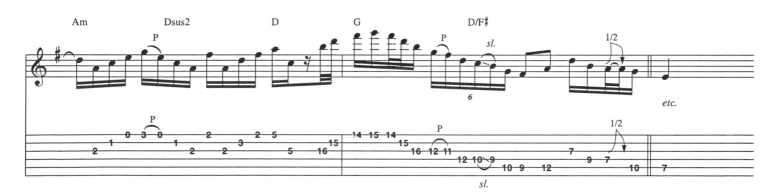

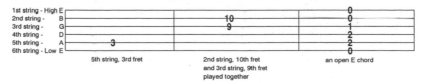

TABLATURE: A six-line staff that graphically represents the guitar fingerboard. By placing a number on the appropriate line, the string and the fret of any note can be indicated. For example:

```
1st string - High E
2nd string -      B                    10              0
3rd string -      G                     9              1
4th string -      D                                    2
5th string -      A          3                         2
6th string - Low E                                     0
```

5th string, 3rd fret   2nd string, 10th fret   an open E chord
and 3rd string, 9th fret
played together

Definitions for Special Guitar Notation

BEND: Strike the note and bend up a half step (one fret).

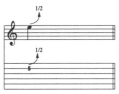

BEND: Strike the note and bend up a whole step (two frets).

BEND AND RELEASE: Strike the note and bend up a half (or whole) step, then release the bend back to the original note. All three notes are tied; only the first note is struck.

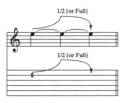

PRE-BEND: Bend the note up a half (or whole) step, then strike it.

PRE-BEND AND RELEASE: Bend the note up a half (or whole) step, strike it and release the bend back to the original note.

UNISON BEND: Strike the two notes simultaneously and bend the lower note to the pitch of the higher.

VIBRATO: Vibrate the note by rapidly bending and releasing the string with a left-hand finger.

WIDE OR EXAGGERATED VIBRATO: Vibrate the pitch to a greater degree with a left-hand finger or the tremolo bar.

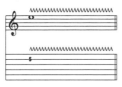

SLIDE: Strike the first note and then with the same left-hand finger move up the string to the second note. The second note is not struck.

SLIDE: Same as above, except the second note is struck.

SLIDE: Slide up to the note indicated from a few frets below.

HAMMER-ON: Strike the first (lower) note, then sound the higher note with another finger by fretting it without picking.

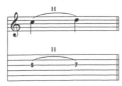

PULL-OFF: Place both fingers on the notes to be sounded. Strike the first (higher) note, then sound the lower note by pulling the finger off the higher note while keeping the lower note fretted.

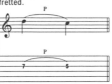

TRILL: Very rapidly alternate between the note indicated and the small note shown in parentheses by hammering on and pulling off.

TAPPING: Hammer ("tap") the fret indicated with the right-hand index or middle finger and pull off to the note fretted by the left hand.

NATURAL HARMONIC: With a left-hand finger, lightly touch the string over the fret indicated, then strike it. A chime-like sound is produced.

ARTIFICIAL HARMONIC: Fret the note normally and sound the harmonic by adding the right-hand thumb edge or index finger tip to the normal pick attack.

A.H. pitch: E

TREMOLO BAR: Drop the note by the number of steps indicated, then return to original pitch.

PALM MUTE: With the right hand, partially mute the note by lightly touching the string just before the bridge.

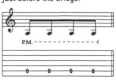

MUFFLED STRINGS: Lay the left hand across the strings without depressing them to the fretboard; strike the strings with the right hand, producing a percussive sound.

PICK SLIDE: Rub the pick edge down the length of the string to produce a scratchy sound.

TREMOLO PICKING: Pick the note as rapidly and continuously as possible.

RHYTHM SLASHES: Strum chords in rhythm indicated. Use chord voicings found in the fingering diagrams at the top of the first page of the transcription.

SINGLE-NOTE RHYTHM SLASHES: The circled number above the note name indicates which string to play. When successive notes are played on the same string, only the fret numbers are given.